I'M BECOMING AN ACE AT MENTAL MATHS!

Ages 6-10

Addition
Subtraction
Multiplication
Division

100 KENDOKU TO SOLVE!

© 2020 Playful Kids Collection
All rights reserved.
ISBN : 9798561888434

90   grids   4 x 4

10   grids   5 x 5

In order to teach pupils the basics of arithmetic, a Japanese teacher came up with an idea to conduct exercises in a playful way similar to Sudoku. These exercises sparked so much excitement among the pupils that this game involving grids called Kendoku ended up having real success in all of Japan, followed by plenty of countries all around the globe!

This book contains 100 grids of Kendoku which will offer children from the age of 6-10 a positive learning experience and will enable them to develop their knowledge of the basics of arithmetic, while having fun at the same time!

How to fill a Kendoku grid ?!

Nothing could be simpler!

1 Find the numbers you need to fill in the grid with!

To do this, you have to count the number of boxes in a row.

In our example, there are 4 boxes. So you will have to use the numbers 1 to 4 to fill the grid.

When you fill out the grid, each of the numbers must appear <u>once per line</u> and <u>once per column</u>!

2 For each area delimited by a BOLD line, find the numbers that go into the boxes!

To do this, you have to find the numbers that give the result indicated at the top left of each zone by using the indicated operator (+,-,x or /)

For example, for our grid we have :

$$3 = 1 + 2 \qquad 7 = 3 + 4 \qquad 6 = 2 \times 3$$
$$12 = 3 \times 4 \qquad 4 = 4 / 1$$
$$9 = 2 + 3 + 4 \qquad 2 = 1 \times 2 \times 1$$

N°1

<table>
<tr><td>1-</td><td></td><td>1-</td><td>3-</td></tr>
<tr><td>2/</td><td></td><td></td><td></td></tr>
<tr><td>48x</td><td></td><td>4+</td><td>1-</td></tr>
<tr><td></td><td></td><td></td><td></td></tr>
</table>

N°2

<table>
<tr><td>6x</td><td></td><td>5+</td><td></td></tr>
<tr><td>1-</td><td>4x</td><td></td><td>9+</td></tr>
<tr><td></td><td>2x</td><td>5+</td><td></td></tr>
<tr><td></td><td></td><td></td><td></td></tr>
</table>

N°3

<table>
<tr><td>4+</td><td>2-</td><td></td><td>1-</td></tr>
<tr><td></td><td>36x</td><td></td><td></td></tr>
<tr><td>8x</td><td></td><td></td><td>12x</td></tr>
<tr><td></td><td>2/</td><td></td><td></td></tr>
</table>

N°4

<table>
<tr><td>4+</td><td></td><td>11+</td><td>3+</td></tr>
<tr><td>9+</td><td></td><td></td><td></td></tr>
<tr><td></td><td>2x</td><td>6+</td><td></td></tr>
<tr><td></td><td></td><td>4+</td><td></td></tr>
</table>

N°5

<table>
<tr><td>18x</td><td>4/</td><td></td><td>3+</td></tr>
<tr><td></td><td></td><td>2/</td><td></td></tr>
<tr><td>4/</td><td></td><td></td><td>12x</td></tr>
<tr><td>6x</td><td></td><td></td><td></td></tr>
</table>

6+		11+	
6x			1-
	3-		
5+		1-	

1-
9+
1-
4+
12x
5+
6x

<table>
<tr><td>6+</td><td>3/</td><td>6+</td><td></td></tr>
<tr><td></td><td></td><td>1-</td><td></td></tr>
<tr><td></td><td>32x</td><td>3/</td><td>2x</td></tr>
<tr><td></td><td></td><td></td><td></td></tr>
</table>

N°9

1-		32x	2-
4+			
	8x	5+	
		5+	

N°11

<table>
<tr><td>9x</td><td></td><td>6+</td><td></td></tr>
<tr><td>2/</td><td></td><td>8x</td><td>4+</td></tr>
<tr><td></td><td></td><td></td><td></td></tr>
<tr><td>2/</td><td></td><td>7+</td><td></td></tr>
</table>

6x	6x		4x
	11+		
		3+	1-
5+			

N°13

<table>
<tr><td>3x</td><td>2/</td><td>32x</td><td></td></tr>
<tr><td></td><td></td><td></td><td>6x</td></tr>
<tr><td>2/</td><td>7+</td><td>5+</td><td></td></tr>
<tr><td></td><td></td><td></td><td></td></tr>
</table>

N°14

17

<table>
<tr><td>1-</td><td></td><td>5+</td><td></td></tr>
<tr><td>4+</td><td>6+</td><td>3+</td><td></td></tr>
<tr><td></td><td></td><td>36x</td><td></td></tr>
<tr><td>7+</td><td></td><td></td><td></td></tr>
</table>

N°16

<table>
<tr><td>2/</td><td></td><td>48x</td><td></td></tr>
<tr><td>3x</td><td></td><td></td><td>3+</td></tr>
<tr><td>10+</td><td>1-</td><td></td><td></td></tr>
<tr><td></td><td></td><td>4+</td><td></td></tr>
</table>

2x | 18x | | 16x
12x | | 3+ |
5+ | | 6x |

N°18

<table>
<tr><td>1-</td><td></td><td>8x</td><td>8+</td></tr>
<tr><td>4/</td><td></td><td></td><td></td></tr>
<tr><td>7+</td><td>4+</td><td></td><td></td></tr>
<tr><td></td><td></td><td>5+</td><td></td></tr>
</table>

N°19

1-

12x

3-

2/

6+

8x

18x

<table>
<tr><td>3/</td><td>2x</td><td>6+</td><td></td></tr>
<tr><td></td><td></td><td>36x</td><td></td></tr>
<tr><td>2/</td><td></td><td>2x</td><td></td></tr>
<tr><td>1-</td><td></td><td></td><td></td></tr>
</table>

N°22

5+ · 16x · 2- · 3+ · 32x · 4+ · 5+

5+		2-	8x
2-			
8x	3-	9x	

6+			16x
18x			
	9+	2/	6x

12x	4x		4/
		3x	
2x	48x		1-

N°26

<table>
<tr><td>2x</td><td>1-</td><td>16x</td><td></td></tr>
<tr><td></td><td></td><td>3x</td><td></td></tr>
<tr><td>48x</td><td></td><td></td><td>1-</td></tr>
<tr><td></td><td>2/</td><td></td><td></td></tr>
</table>

4x

12x

5+

4+

11+

6x

3+

N°28

5+

7+

36x

3-

2x

6x

4/

31

2x
1-
1-
11+
4+
4x
1-

N°31

4+		7+	
24x		32x	3/
	6+		

3+		36x	
6x	4/	8x	
			2x
12x			

N°33

5+		7+	4x
4+			
	48x	3+	5+

N°34

<table>
<tr><td>1-</td><td>3+</td><td></td><td>4/</td></tr>
<tr><td></td><td>1-</td><td>3-</td><td></td></tr>
<tr><td>16x</td><td></td><td></td><td>18x</td></tr>
<tr><td></td><td></td><td></td><td></td></tr>
</table>

3x

8x

9+

11+

2/

2/

4+

N°36

<table>
<tr><td>3x</td><td></td><td>6+</td><td>1-</td></tr>
<tr><td></td><td>2/</td><td></td><td></td></tr>
<tr><td>8x</td><td></td><td>3/</td><td></td></tr>
<tr><td></td><td>6+</td><td></td><td></td></tr>
</table>

3+

12x

8x

7+

5+

1-

3x

<table>
<tr><td>9x</td><td></td><td>3-</td><td>6+</td></tr>
<tr><td>2/</td><td></td><td></td><td></td></tr>
<tr><td></td><td>7+</td><td>5+</td><td>3x</td></tr>
<tr><td></td><td></td><td></td><td></td></tr>
</table>

N°39

<table>
<tr><td>2/</td><td></td><td>36x</td><td>3-</td></tr>
<tr><td>1-</td><td></td><td></td><td></td></tr>
<tr><td></td><td>9+</td><td>2x</td><td>1-</td></tr>
<tr><td></td><td></td><td></td><td></td></tr>
</table>

4+ 7+ 2-

6x 8+

6+ 4+

N°41

<table>
<tr><td>1-</td><td>3/</td><td>48x</td><td></td></tr>
<tr><td></td><td></td><td></td><td>2/</td></tr>
<tr><td>7+</td><td>6+</td><td></td><td></td></tr>
<tr><td></td><td>6x</td><td></td><td></td></tr>
</table>

<table>
<tr><td>6x</td><td>12x</td><td>4+</td><td></td></tr>
<tr><td></td><td></td><td></td><td>2/</td></tr>
<tr><td>4/</td><td>4+</td><td></td><td></td></tr>
<tr><td></td><td>9+</td><td></td><td></td></tr>
</table>

5+

12x

3-

1-

7+

4+

1-

N°44

48x

2x

1-

2x

7+

4/

1-

2/

5+

12x

4/

48x

5+

1-

<table>
<tr><td>9+</td><td></td><td></td><td>2x</td></tr>
<tr><td>7+</td><td>1-</td><td></td><td></td></tr>
<tr><td></td><td></td><td>9+</td><td></td></tr>
<tr><td></td><td>4+</td><td></td><td></td></tr>
</table>

9+

2x

11+

6+

4+

7+

3+

11+

1-

1-

12x

4/

6+

5+	3x	2-	
		48x	3+
3-			
	6+		

N°50

6x	3/		9+
	2x		
4x		18x	
	8x		

N°52

<table>
<tr><td>6x</td><td>2/</td><td></td><td>7+</td></tr>
<tr><td></td><td>7+</td><td></td><td></td></tr>
<tr><td>5+</td><td>6+</td><td>9x</td><td></td></tr>
<tr><td></td><td></td><td></td><td></td></tr>
</table>

N°54

2/	36x		3-
	8x		
7+		2x	
		1-	

N°55

<table>
<tr><td>9x</td><td></td><td>2/</td><td>8+</td></tr>
<tr><td>8x</td><td></td><td></td><td></td></tr>
<tr><td></td><td>2x</td><td></td><td></td></tr>
<tr><td>3-</td><td></td><td>1-</td><td></td></tr>
</table>

N°56

<table>
<tr><td>1-</td><td>12x</td><td></td><td>4/</td></tr>
<tr><td></td><td></td><td>1-</td><td></td></tr>
<tr><td>4/</td><td>2/</td><td></td><td>18x</td></tr>
<tr><td></td><td></td><td></td><td></td></tr>
</table>

6+
11+
3+
6+
3/
1-
2x

<table>
<tr><td>12x</td><td></td><td>3x</td><td>2/</td></tr>
<tr><td>8x</td><td></td><td></td><td></td></tr>
<tr><td></td><td>2/</td><td></td><td>4+</td></tr>
<tr><td></td><td>1-</td><td></td><td></td></tr>
</table>

N°59

<table>
<tr><td>4+</td><td></td><td>7+</td><td></td></tr>
<tr><td>24x</td><td></td><td>8x</td><td></td></tr>
<tr><td></td><td>5+</td><td></td><td>4+</td></tr>
<tr><td></td><td>4x</td><td></td><td></td></tr>
</table>

1-	3x	7+	
		6+	
4/			9x
2/			

4+

8x

2/

1-

6+

32x

3x

N°62

N°64

<table>
<tr><td>1-</td><td>1-</td><td>48x</td><td></td></tr>
<tr><td></td><td></td><td></td><td>2/</td></tr>
<tr><td>12x</td><td>3-</td><td></td><td></td></tr>
<tr><td></td><td>6x</td><td></td><td></td></tr>
</table>

2x	6x		8x
	36x	4/	
5+		5+	

N°66

2/

9+

8x

36x

6+

4x

N°68

2-	7+		1-
	2-		
8x		9x	1-

N°70

6+

5+

5+

4/

48x

5+

2/

<table>
<tr><td>2/</td><td>7+</td><td></td><td>4x</td></tr>
<tr><td></td><td>6x</td><td></td><td></td></tr>
<tr><td>11+</td><td></td><td>2/</td><td></td></tr>
<tr><td></td><td>6x</td><td></td><td></td></tr>
</table>

<table>
<tr><td>6x</td><td>3+</td><td>12x</td><td></td></tr>
<tr><td></td><td></td><td>2-</td><td></td></tr>
<tr><td></td><td>48x</td><td></td><td>6+</td></tr>
<tr><td></td><td></td><td></td><td></td></tr>
</table>

5+

5+

1-

7+

4+

24x

7+

9x		7+	8+
	8x		
6+			
	6+		

1-		4x	
48x			24x
2x		6+	

N°76

18x

5+

7+

6x

3+

5+

12x

N°77

9+

4/

7+

2/

2x

7+

6x

80

N°78

1- 11+   2/

3+

4x 3+   36x

3x

6+

7+

1-

3x

8x

6x

2-		8x	
6x	32x		
		3/	
4/		6x	

1- 1-   2x

8x

1- 1-

4x

5+	3-		8x
	7+		
3+		18x	
4x			

N°83

5+ · 2/ 3-
7+ 4+
5+
12x

86

N°84

N°85

N°86

3+
12x
4x
6x
48x
4+
1-

89

N°87

N°88

N°89

9x | 3+ | | 7+
 | | 12x |
6+ | | |
4/ | | 1- |

18x

4x

2x

9+

9+

6x

<table>
<tr><td>12x</td><td></td><td></td><td>10x</td><td></td></tr>
<tr><td>40x</td><td></td><td>1-</td><td></td><td>3x</td></tr>
<tr><td></td><td>2/</td><td>8+</td><td>3x</td><td></td></tr>
<tr><td>6+</td><td></td><td></td><td></td><td>80x</td></tr>
<tr><td></td><td>1-</td><td></td><td></td><td></td></tr>
</table>

N°92

N°93

2x | 48x | | 12+ |
| 3/ | | 10x |
12+ | | | | 3/
| 10x | 2- | |
| | | 12x |

<table>
<tr><td>20x</td><td></td><td>6x</td><td></td><td></td></tr>
<tr><td>12+</td><td></td><td>7+</td><td></td><td>4/</td></tr>
<tr><td></td><td>5+</td><td>5+</td><td>15x</td><td></td></tr>
<tr><td>4+</td><td></td><td></td><td></td><td>10x</td></tr>
<tr><td></td><td></td><td>1-</td><td></td><td></td></tr>
</table>

N°96

N°97

4+

2-

9+

6+

10x

12x

4+

15x

13+

1-

2x

N°99

6+		2-		4+
5+	12x	5/		
			9+	
11+		6x		12x
		6+		

N°100

6+ 6+ 7+ 30x

4+

3/ 8x 14+

2/

2- 7+

103

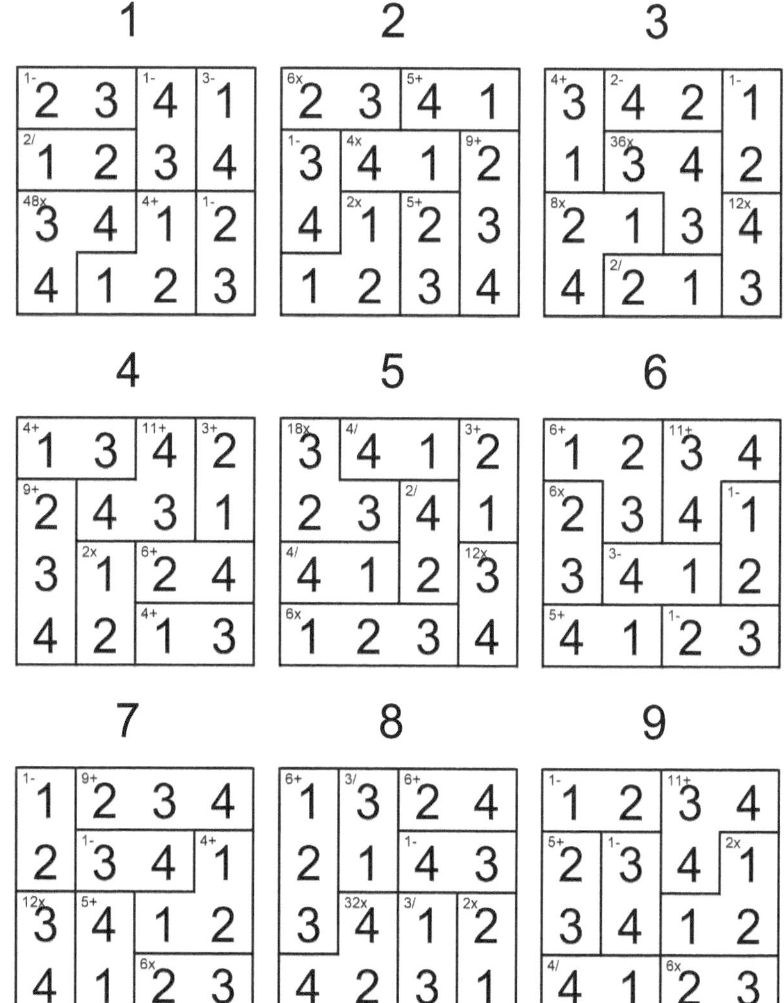

10

1- 2	3	32x 4	2- 1
4+ 1	4	2	3
3	8x 2	5+ 1	4
4	1	5+ 3	2

11

9x 3	1	6+ 4	2
2/ 4	3	8x 2	4+ 1
2	4	1	3
2/ 1	2	7+ 3	4

12

6x 1	6x 2	3	4x 4
2	11+ 3	4	1
3	4	3+ 1	1- 2
5+ 4	1	2	3

13

3x 3	2/ 1	32x 2	4
1	2	4	6x 3
2/ 4	7+ 3	5+ 1	2
2	4	3	1

14

6x 3	1	32x 2	4
3+ 1	2	4	4+ 3
2	48x 4	6+ 3	1
4	3	1	2

15

1- 2	3	5+ 4	1
4+ 3	6+ 4	3+ 1	2
1	2	36x 3	4
7+ 4	1	2	3

16

2/ 1	2	48x 3	4
3x 3	1	4	3+ 2
10+ 4	1- 3	2	1
2	4	4+ 1	3

17

2x 1	18x 2	3	16x 4
2	3	4	1
12x 3	4	3+ 1	2
5+ 4	1	6x 2	3

18

1- 2	3	8x 4	8+ 1
4/ 1	4	2	3
7+ 3	4+ 2	1	4
4	1	5+ 3	2

19

3	1	2	4
4	3	1	2
1	2	4	3
2	4	3	1

20

2	3	1	4
3	4	2	1
1	2	4	3
4	1	3	2

21

3	1	4	2
1	2	3	4
2	4	1	3
4	3	2	1

22

2	3	4	1
3	1	2	4
1	4	3	2
4	2	1	3

23

3	2	4	1
1	3	2	4
4	1	3	2
2	4	1	3

24

1	2	3	4
2	3	4	1
3	4	1	2
4	1	2	3

25

3	1	2	4
4	2	3	1
2	4	1	3
1	3	4	2

26

2	3	4	1
1	2	3	4
3	4	1	2
4	1	2	3

27

2	1	3	4
3	2	4	1
1	4	2	3
4	3	1	2

28

5+1	2	7+3	4
2	36x3	3-4	1
3	4	2x1	6x2
4/4	1	2	3

29

3+1	1-3	2	48x4
2	8+1	4	3
3	4	2/1	2
2/4	2	2-3	1

30

2x1	2	1-3	4
1-2	11+3	4	4+1
3	4	1	2
4x4	1	1-2	3

31

4+1	2	7+3	4
24x2	1	32x4	3/3
3	4	2	1
4	6+3	1	2

32

3+1	2	36x3	4
6x2	4/1	8x4	3
3	4	2	2x1
12x4	3	1	2

33

5+2	1	7+3	4x4
4+3	2	4	1
1	48x4	3+2	5+3
4	3	1	2

34

1-3	3+1	2	4/4
2	1-3	3-4	1
16x4	2	1	18x3
1	4	3	2

35

3x1	3	8x2	4
9+2	11+4	3	2/1
3	2/1	4	2
4	2	4+1	3

36

3x3	1	6+2	1-4
1	2/2	4	3
8x2	4	3/3	1
4	6+3	1	2

37

3+	12x		8x
1	3	4	2
2	7+ 1	5+ 3	4
1- 3	4	2	3x 1
4	2	1	3

38

9x		3-	6+
3	1	4	2
2/ 2	3	1	4
4	7+ 2	5+ 3	3x 1
1	4	2	3

39

2/		36x	3-
1	2	3	4
1- 2	3	4	1
3	9+ 4	2x 1	1- 2
4	1	2	3

40

4+	7+	2-	
1	3	4	2
3	4	6x 2	8+ 1
6+ 2	4+ 1	3	4
4	2	1	3

41

1-	3/	48x	
2	1	3	4
1	3	4	2/ 2
7+ 3	6+ 4	2	1
4	6x 2	1	3

42

6x	12x	4+	
3	4	2	1
2	3	1	2/ 4
4/ 4	4+ 1	3	2
1	9+ 2	4	3

43

5+		12x	3-
1	2	3	4
2	1- 3	4	1
7+ 3	4	4+ 1	1- 2
4	1	2	3

44

48x		2x	1-
3	4	1	2
4	2x 1	2	3
1	2	7+ 3	4/ 4
1- 2	3	4	1

45

2/	5+	12x	
1	2	3	4
2	3	4/ 4	1
48x 3	4	1	5+ 2
4	1- 1	2	3

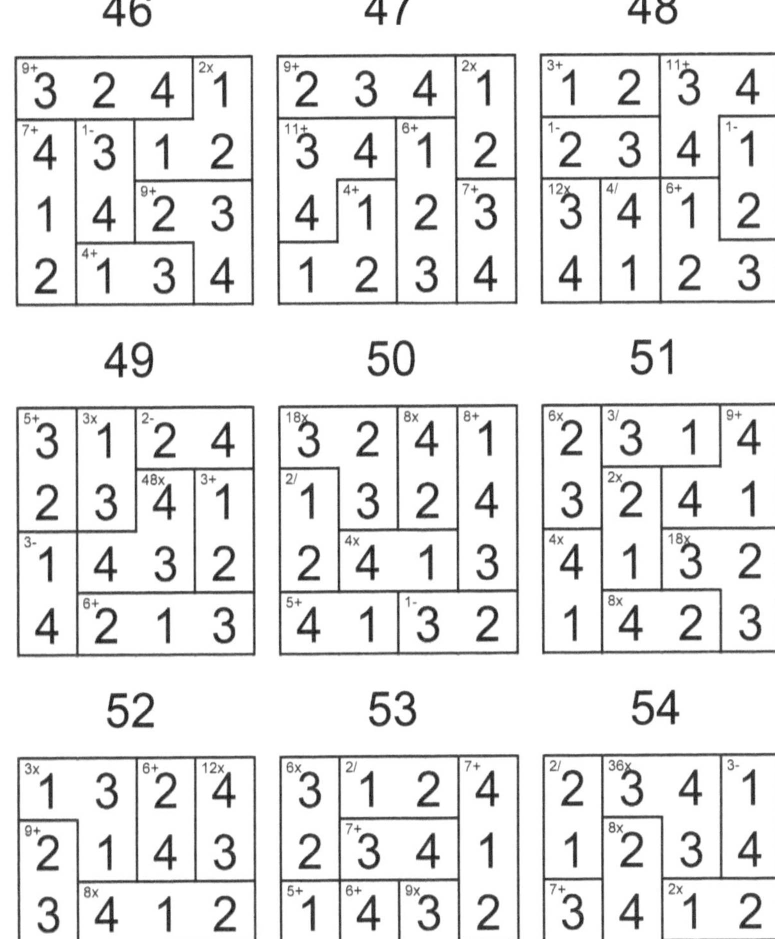

55

9x 3	1	2/ 2	8+ 4
8x 2	3	4	1
4	2x 2	1	3
3- 1	4	1- 3	2

56

1- 2	12x 3	4	4/ 1
3	1	1- 2	4
4/ 4	2/ 2	1	18x 3
1	4	3	2

57

6+ 3	1	2	11+ 4
3+ 1	6+ 2	4	3
2	4	3/ 3	1
1- 4	3	2x 1	2

58

12x 3	4	3x 1	2/ 2
8x 2	1	3	4
1	2/ 2	4	4+ 3
4	1- 3	2	1

59

4+ 1	2	7+ 3	4
24x 3	1	8x 4	2
4	5+ 3	2	4+ 1
2	4x 4	1	3

60

1- 2	3x 3	7+ 1	4
3	1	6+ 4	2
4/ 1	4	2	9x 3
2/ 4	2	3	1

61

4+ 3	1	8x 2	4
2/ 1	2	1- 4	6+ 3
32x 2	4	3	1
4	3x 3	1	2

62

6x 1	2	3	6+ 4
1- 3	3- 1	4	2
2	11+ 4	2x 1	3/ 3
4	3	2	1

63

4+ 3	1	6+ 2	4
9+ 4	2	3	1- 1
1- 1	48x 3	4	2
2	4	3/ 1	3

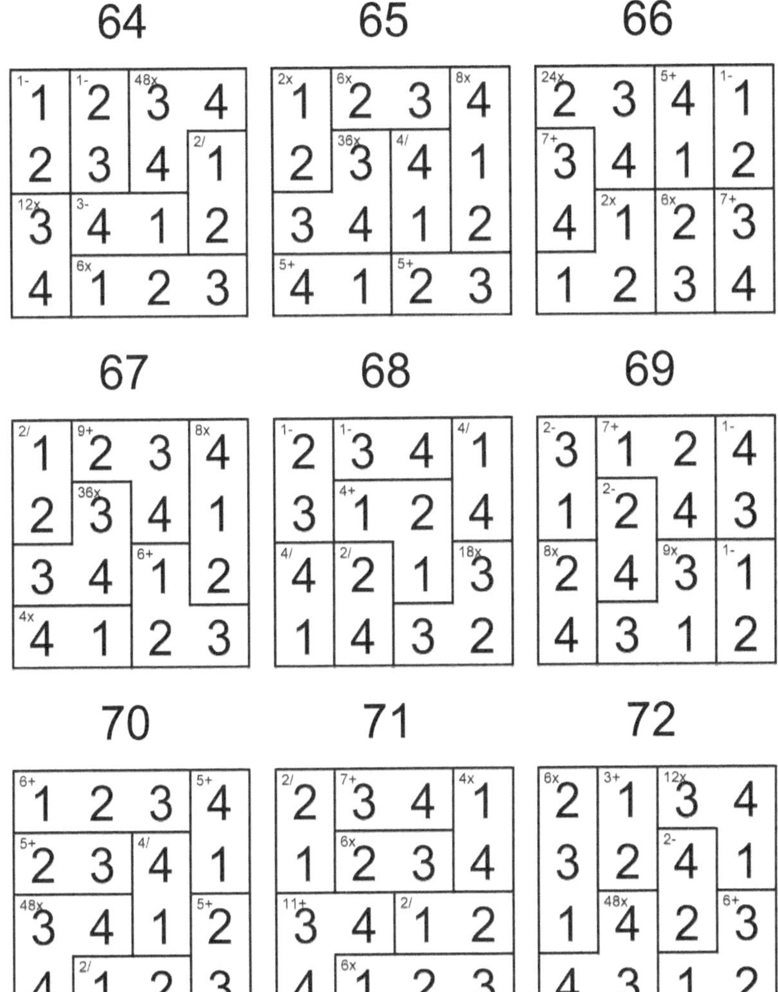

73

5+ 3	2	5+ 4	1- 1
7+ 4	3	1	2
4+ 2	1	24x 3	7+ 4
1	4	2	3

74

9x 1	3	7+ 2	8+ 4
3	8x 2	4	1
6+ 2	4	1	3
4	6+ 1	3	2

75

1- 3	2	4x 4	1
48x 4	3	1	24x 2
2x 1	4	6+ 2	3
2	1	3	4

76

18x 3	2	5+ 1	4
7+ 4	3	6x 2	3+ 1
1	5+ 4	3	2
2	1	12x 4	3

77

9+ 2	3	4/ 1	4
7+ 3	4	2/ 2	1
4	2x 1	7+ 3	6x 2
1	2	4	3

78

1- 2	11+ 3	4	2/ 1
3	4	3+ 1	2
4x 4	3+ 1	2	36x 3
1	2	3	4

79

3x 3	1	6+ 2	4
7+ 2	1- 3	4	3x 1
4	8x 2	1	3
1	4	6x 3	2

80

2- 1	3	8x 2	4
6x 3	32x 2	4	1
2	4	3/ 1	3
4/ 4	1	6x 3	2

81

1- 2	1- 3	4	2x 1
3	8x 4	1	2
1	2	1- 3	1- 4
4x 4	1	2	3

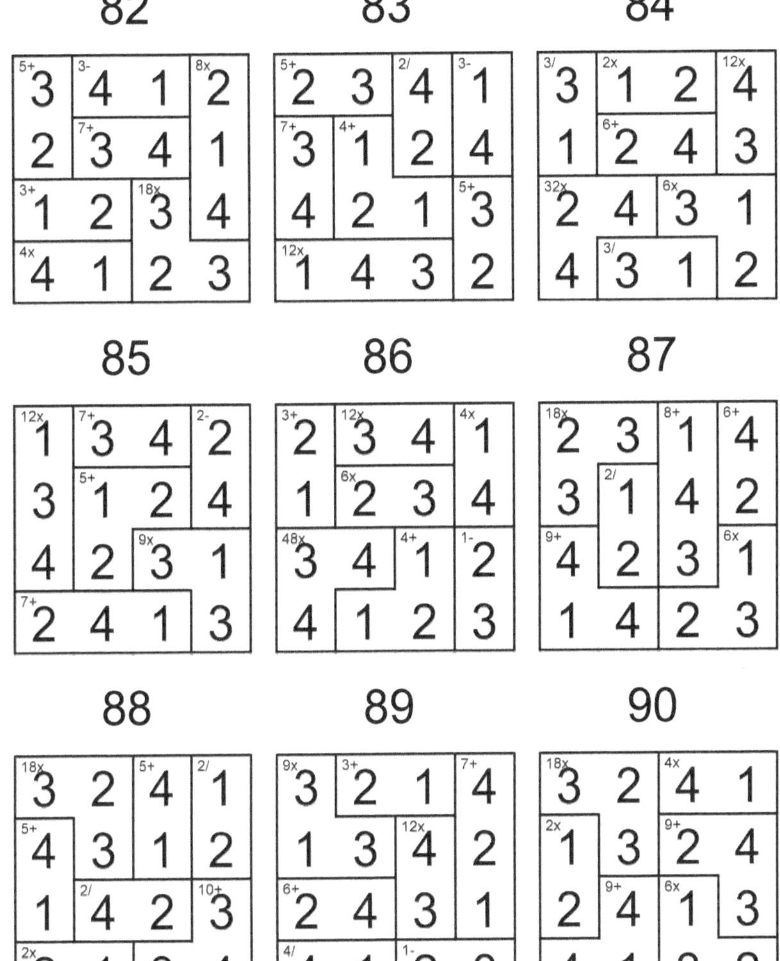

91

3	1	4	5	2
4	5	1	2	3
2	4	5	3	1
5	2	3	1	4
1	3	2	4	5

92

4	2	3	5	1
1	4	5	2	3
2	5	1	3	4
3	1	2	4	5
5	3	4	1	2

93

3	1	4	5	2
4	5	3	2	1
1	2	5	3	4
5	4	2	1	3
2	3	1	4	5

94

1	4	3	5	2
2	3	4	1	5
4	1	5	2	3
3	5	2	4	1
5	2	1	3	4

95

4	5	2	1	3
3	4	5	2	1
5	2	1	3	4
1	3	4	5	2
2	1	3	4	5

96

1	3	2	4	5
2	4	3	5	1
4	2	5	1	3
3	5	1	2	4
5	1	4	3	2

97

4	1	5	2	3
3	4	1	5	2
1	2	3	4	5
2	5	4	3	1
5	3	2	1	4

98

1	2	3	4	5
4	1	5	2	3
2	3	1	5	4
5	4	2	3	1
3	5	4	1	2

99

4	2	3	5	1
3	4	5	1	2
2	3	1	4	5
5	1	2	3	4
1	5	4	2	3

100

⁶⁺4	⁶⁺5	1	⁷⁺3	^{30x}2
2	⁴⁺1	3	4	5
^{3/}1	^{8x}2	¹⁴⁺4	5	3
3	4	5	^{2/}2	1
²⁻5	3	⁷⁺2	1	4

www.ingramcontent.com/pod-product-compliance
Lightning Source LLC
Chambersburg PA
CBHW020118180726
47992CB00019B/860